sponsored by Andrews McMeel Universal and Follett College Stores

STRIP SEARCH

sponsored by Andrews McMeel Universal and Follett College Stores

Revealing Today's Best College Cartoonists

Andrews McMeel
Publishing

Kansas City

www.andrewsmcmeel.com and www.uexpress.com

99 00 01 02 03 BAH 10 9 8 7 6 5 4 3 2 1

ISBN: 0-8362-8343-0

Library of Congress Catalog Card Number: 98-88678

Cover illustration by
Jan Thomas, Brett Schroeder, Tony Morris, Ray Lancon, and Stephen Emond.

Acknowledgments:

p. 13 Excerpt, Flashbacks © 1995 G. B. Trudeau.
Reprinted with permission.

p. 36 Excerpt, Camp FoxTrot © 1998 Bill Amend.
Reprinted with permission.

Foreword

It's fun going through a stack of submissions many inches thick. In the case of the several hundred packages we received for the first Strip Search contest, serendipity informed us and we editors who reviewed the material were hoping for surprises in the form of humor, characters, and art. And find those we did.

The criteria we use in selecting comic panels or strips are difficult to delineate—a comic sometimes appeals to one editor and not to another. But I believe our selections in this book share some common elements:
- We tend to favor good writing over good art (but we like good art).
- We tend to favor the cartoonist who is adventurous in writing or concept.
- We tend to favor work influenced by another's over work that is derivative, and we tend to favor the sui generis over work that is influenced.

Always, of course, we were mindful that most of these applicants were students and that art often needs time to mature. And we were also mindful that what works in a college setting—or what appeals to college readers—might not in a larger market.

We hope you'll find fun in reading these. Keep in mind that these are relative choices, selected in relation to the others we received.

If you think we erred, let us know. Or even better, send your own work in next time!
                                        —Lee Salem, Editorial Director, Universal Press Syndicate

Grand Prize Winner

Stephen Emond
Middlesex Community Technical College
Madison, Connecticut

Dear Diary, I think I'm in love. My days are filled with sunshine, the birds are singing, its like everything I've heard love is.

...So you can expect plenty of tears from me soon.

11

Panel Cartoon Category

September 30, 1968

Bull Tales, by G.B. Trudeau, first appears in *Yale Daily News* and within a few weeks attracts the attention of Universal Press Syndicate co-founder and editor, James F. Andrews.

October 26, 1970

Renamed after its principal character, *Doonesbury* debuts in 28 newspapers.

"I was approached about syndication during my junior year in college, after an arduous four-week apprenticeship on the school paper. Incredibly, the offer didn't strike me as particularly remarkable. It was the very essence of being in the right place at the right time, but when you're young, you don't understand serendipity. You feel entitled, even to your accidents."

—Garry Trudeau, *Doonesbury* creator

1st Place Winner

Jacob M. Lightbody
Orange Coast College
Costa Mesa, California

Free as a bird

Larry offers a toast to the spirit of Manifest Destiny.

Mrs. Phelps finds difficulty in breaking away from familiar routines.

Mort loves to drive with the top down and feel the breeze blow through his hair.

It is doubtful that truth in advertising would actually prove to be refreshing.

Walter finds discontent in being provided the opportunity to exercise personal freedom.

Ray Lancon
University of Southern California
Los Angeles, California

Scrabble in hell.

How Expressions Are Formed

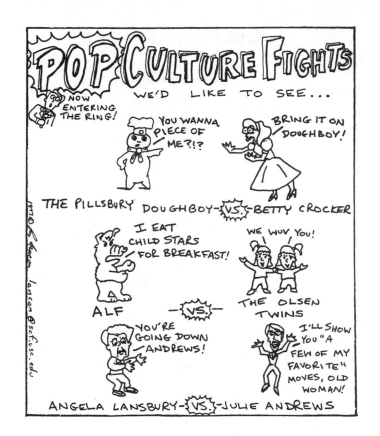

"Sellout."

20

Professor Stillfield had spent years trying to answer that one nagging question: How do you solve a problem like Maria?

Aliens study Earth fashion.

Eventually Medusa was just deemed
an unfit mother.

**Until it was later changed to a pea, the story of
"The Princess and the Spike" never really
caught on.**

3rd Place Winner

Tony Morris
Lawrence Technological University
Southfield, Michigan

Goofing off at the Solitaire Development Company

Suddenly, the rest of the clan realized why Gronk was such a good hunter—he was using an illegally corked club.

Cat bathroom

It was times like this that Spot Johnson wished
he had been housebroken.

Honorable Mention

Jan Thomas
New Mexico Tech
Socorro, New Mexico

ALL WAS QUIET EXCEPT FOR THE STIFLED GASP OF THE DENTIST AND THE NERVOUS RUSTLING OF THE HYGIENIST. BOB KNEW IT WAS GOING TO BE A BAD AFTERNOON.

FRANK COULDN'T FIGURE OUT WHY HE WAS SO SHORT ON HIS WALNUT DELUXE INVENTORY.

BACK IN CHICAGO, THE FAMILY WAS STILL PUZZLED
BY THE SIMULTANEOUS DISSAPEARANCE OF THE
CAT AND THE CREDIT CARDS.

THE EDITORS AT WORK

THE EDITOR

DON'T ABANDON YOUR
POT BELLIED PIG!

Needless to SAY, the CHEERFUL LiTTle tune WAS UNappreciAted.

Forces OF Nature

tornado

eARthquake

MotheR Didn't get heR MotheRS DAY card.

Other Cartoons

Most every comic strip you see in a newspaper anymore is distributed by a handful of companies called syndicates (don't let the word fool you—they're much scarier than they sound). This means that before a cartoonist can seriously hope to see his or her comic strip in a newspaper, he or she must first land a deal with one of these syndicates, which is no easy task. Thousands and thousands of comic strip submissions from aspiring professional and amateur cartoonists arrive in syndicate offices by mail over the course of each year, from which each syndicate chooses at most two or three to distribute. It took me nearly three years of submitting and resubmitting various batches of *FoxTrot*—as an unpublished amateur straight out of college—before Universal Press Syndicate offered me a contract in 1987.

—Bill Amend, creator of *FoxTrot*

1st Place

David Krantz (nom de plume: p. cinnamon)
Rutgers University
New Brunswick, New Jersey

Self-hating blackbirds often burn crosses in the nests of others.

sOAP sCUM
by p. cinnamon

Richard froze. He knew he'd gambled away his mother's panties for the last time. "Not the harness," he thought. "Please, Mama, not the harness."

"But if I don't raise taxes then how could we ever afford to lower them?"

"Yes, I agree. He'll make a fine gimp, indeed."

"While it was very kind of you, indeed, to help the lady cross the street, the penalty for abetted jaywalking is death."

**In his college days, Jesus
was affectionately called "Jiz"
by his peers.**

2nd Place

Josh R. Rose
University of North Texas
Denton, Texas

COSMO "INTROSPECTION"

© 1998 J. ROSE

by: JOSH ROSE

C · O · S · M · O

"PHILOSOPHY"

by: JOSH "KING OF SELF DEPRECATION" ROSE   © 1988-1998 J. ROSE

YET ANOTHER BLIND DATE...

BEMUSED SMILE

GOOD POSTURE

SALAD

THIN SANDWICH

NERVOUS RAMBLING

ELBOWS ON TABLE.

...AND I'M A QUARTER POLISH, AND AN ART STUDENT, ALTHOUGH I DO HOPE TO GET MY MASTERS DEGREE IN ART HISTORY, AND I LIKE KEVIN SMITH AND HAL HARTLEY FILMS, AND I CAN'T COOK, BUT I CAN MAKE PRETTY GOOD TOAST, AND, AND, I'VE NEVER TRIED TO COMMIT SUICIDE— EXCEPT THAT ONE TIME, BUT I WAS DRUNK AND THE HAIR GREW BACK, EXCEPT ON MY BACK, THANK GOD! AND I'M NOT SOME AXE-WIELDING PSYCHO OR ANYTHING— ALTHOUGH I HAVE BEEN TOLD THAT I'M PRETTY DEADLY WITH A PAIR OF NAIL CLIPPERS... I ALSO HAVE A REALLY GOOD OUTLOOK ON LIFE!

SO— WHAT IS YOUR OUTLOOK ON LIFE?

ESSENTIALLY, I VIEW THE WORLD AS A HUGE DUNG BEETLE— AND I'M A PIECE OF DUNG.

AH.

tap

REMINDING HERSELF TO BUY NEW SHOELACES

SO, IS THAT MORE OF A NIETZSCHIAN OR A DESCARTIAN PHILOSOPHY?

IT'S MOSTLY A CHARLIE BROWNIAN PHILOSOPHY.

SILVERWARE SCULPTURE

CHOOSING THE WEDDING COLORS

THAT "IN LIKE FLYNN" POSE

C · O · S · M · O

"BACKGROUND NOISE"

by: Josh "Madness" Rose   © 1988-1998 J. Rose

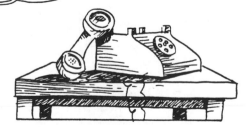

C · O · S · M · O

"KARMIC FLATULENCE"

by: Josh "Poster Child" Rose   COSMO ©1988-1998 J. Rose

COSMO "CHIVALRY"

© COPYRIGHT 1998 by: Josh Rose

COSMO   "The Reality of Charts"

© COPYRIGHT 1998   by: JOSH ROSE

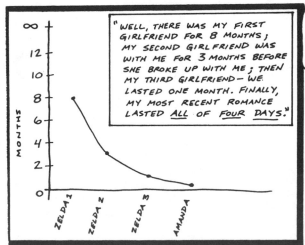

3rd Place

Matthew Wiegle
Yale University
New Haven, Connecticut

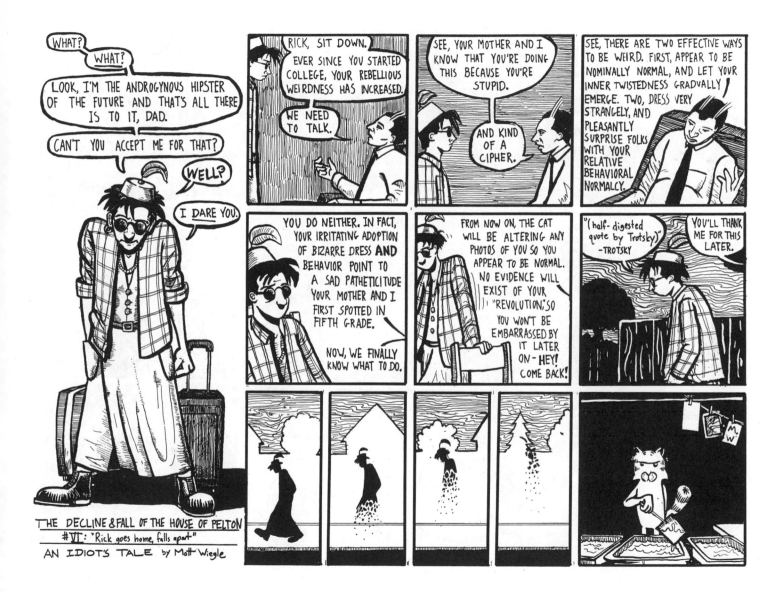

THE DECLINE & FALL OF THE HOUSE OF PELTON
#VI: "Rick goes home, falls apart"
AN IDIOT'S TALE by Matt Wiegle

Honorable Mention

C. Haun
Cypress College
Cypress, California

SIXES & SEVENS

I AM THE GREAT AND ALL-KNOWING SWAMI!!© I LOOK DEEP INTO THE UNKNOWN REACHES OF SPACE AND TIME AND PULL FROM ITS DEPTHS ANSWERS TO DILEMMA'S THAT HAVE PLAGUED THE MINDS OF MAN SINCE THE DAWN OF EXISTENCE!! ...AND NOW THE QUOTE OF THE DAY... "WITHIN EVERY BELIEF,... THERE IS A LIE."

UM,... I DISAGREE MR. SWAMI. IF SOMEONE BELIEVES SOMETHING TO BE TRUE YET THEY ALSO BELIEVE IN YOUR THEORY, THEY'RE SYSTEM OF BELIEFS IS PARADOXICAL. NO ONE IN A PROPER STATE OF HUMAN BELIEF CAN SINCERELY BELIEVE IN SOMETHING IF THEY KNOW IT TO BE FALSE. FOR IF ONE PART IS FALSE, THE REST OF IT WHICH IS OBVIOUSLY BASED ON ALL OTHER PARTS, INCLUDING THE FALSE ONE, IS FALSE AS WELL. THEREFORE, THAT PERSON CEASES TO BELIEVE IN ANYTHING AND THEN WOULD SLIP INTO A CHAOTIC REALM OF REASONING WHICH WOULD RENDER ALL OF THEIR BELIEFS EQUIVALENT TO THAT OF THE MERE BABBLING OF A TWO-YEAR OLD CHILD,... MEANINGLESS TO OUR STATE OF THOUGHT AND BEING.

DEDICATED TO: JOSEPH MCCARTHY

THANK YOU MY LITTLE, UH... IMP-LIKE CREATURE...

I'M A FALLEN ANGEL AND MY NAME IS ROBO.

WHATEVER,... YOUR MISSING THE GREAT SWAMI COMPLETELY. "WITHIN EVERY BELIEF THERE IS A LIE." IT'S AS SIMPLE AS THAT! JUST LOOK AT THE FACTS!!

BUT WITH MY ANSWER I'VE BLOWN YOUR THEORY OUT OF THE WATER...

LISTEN TO ME!! IT'S RIGHT THERE!! LOOK AT IT!! IT IS TRUE!!!

...HERE,...WE'LL SPELL IT! B-E-L-I-E-F!! IT'S RIGHT THERE!!...

THE GREAT... SWAMI!!

HE KNOWS ALL!!

I'M GOING TO UNPLUG YOU NOW...

6's & 7's

by: c. haun

Magic Mirror Series: Part 1

Dedicated to: Harry Houdini

Cartoon Strip Category

When you are a professional cartoonist constantly doing battle with deadlines and projects, it's sometimes easy to lose sight of the passion and thrill that drives one into this vocation—a passion and thrill so many aspiring cartoonists seem to exhibit as effortlessly as breathing. Their doodlings are fresh and creative. Like a real-life Calvin at the controls of an F-14 Tomcat, they test-fly their pens and pencils at breakneck speed. Sometimes they get blown out of the sky into a million pieces . . . but more often than not they get right back into the cockpit and take off on another sortie into the boundless stratosphere of comedy and tragedy, often pushing the envelope of both. But possessing confidence and determination should also be tempered with humility and patience. Even Mark McGwire doesn't hit a home run every time he's at the plate.

The younger cartoonist has to be both student and coach. Observing the current talented lineup as well as the ghosts of the past. Learning, absorbing, challenging one's self. Getting knocked down and getting back up again . . . so that even on a day one goes 0 for 4 it can still be considered a success if one learns from it.

As a college cartoonist at Ohio State University I was extremely eager to make my living drawing cartoons. I was excited every time I was published. Nobody likes to hear negative comments, but if it was directed at one of my cartoons it meant someone actually took the time to look at it. I still love what I'm doing . . . maybe even more than I know . . . and I want to thank every one of the entrants of *Strip Search* for refreshing my memory for that passion and thrill that is cartooning. Oops, gotta run. Got another deadline approaching.

—Brian Basset, creator of *Adam@home*

1st Place

Brett Schroeder
Ringling School of Art and Design
Sarasota, Florida

2nd Place

Tony Morris
Lawrence Technological University
Southfield, Michigan

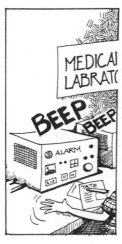

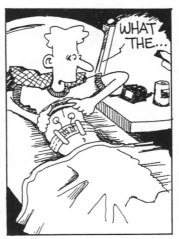

3rd Place

Michael Jones and Alan Davy
Ouachita Baptist University
Arkadelphia, Arkansas
Campbell University
Bules Creek, North Carolina

Honorable Mention

Eric Jones
Syracuse University
Syracuse, New York

Runners-Up

I think that all cartoonists strive to come up with that one perfect cartoon—one that will make every person who reads it laugh out loud. That cartoon does not exist and never will. What people laugh at in a cartoon is a reflection of their own experiences, all of which are far too diverse to be boiled down into twelve square inches of newsprint. We know this, yet we continue to blindly hunt for that elusive Perfect Cartoon. And I think that's what makes this job so much fun.
—John McPherson, creator of *Close to Home*

Destin Berthelot
Rollins College
Winter Park, Florida

David J. Kellett
University of Kent
Canterbury, England

JOHNNY HAD HIT EVERY FLYING SQUIRREL'S
WORST NIGHTMARE: UPDRAFT.

THOR: GOD OF THUNDER, LOKI: GOD OF MISCHIEF,
ERNESTO: GOD IN HIS OWN MIND.

Dan Lee
University of Southern California
Los Angeles, California

Mike McBeth
Florida State University
Tallahassee, Florida

Andrew Micco
Virginia Commonwealth University
Richmond, Virginia

Kevin K. Neidlinger
Georgetown University
Washington, DC

Cathy Nolan
School of Visual Arts
New York, New York

Donny Fort
San Jacinto College
Pasadena, Texas

Kyle Harabedian
Kendall College of Art and Design
Grand Rapids, Michigan

Jessica Wu
Massachusetts Institute of Technology
Cambridge, Massachusetts

Victor Hernandez
San Diego State University
San Diego, California

Ted Dawson
University of the Incarnate Word
San Antonio, Texas